CHECK IT OUT!

LIGHT & SOUND

by Clint Twist

Consultants: Linda McGuigan and Professor Terry Russell
Center for Research in Primary Science and Technology, University of Liverpool

Library of Congress Cataloging-in-Publication Data

Twist, Clint.
    Light & sound / by Clint Twist.
        p. cm. — (Check it out!)
    Includes index.
    ISBN 1-59716-060-1 (lib. bdg.) — ISBN 1-59716-097-0 (pbk.)
    1. Light—Juvenile literature. 2. Light—Experiments—Juvenile literature. 3. Light—Speed—Juvenile literature.
    4. Sound—Juvenile literature. 5. Sound—Experiments—Juvenile literature. 6. Sound—Speed—Juvenile literature.
    I. Title: Light and sound. II. Title. III. Series.

    QC360.T85 2006
    535—dc22

                                    2005008417

For more information, write to Bearport Publishing Company, Inc., 101 Fifth Avenue, Suite 6R, New York, New York 10003. Printed in the United States of America.

1 2 3 4 5 6 7 8 9 10

Contents

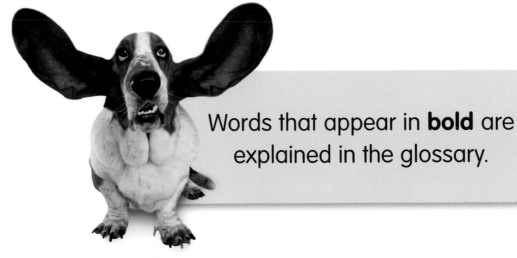

Words that appear in **bold** are explained in the glossary.

Sunlight

Light is **energy** that we can see. During the day, we get **natural** light from the sun. This light is called **sunlight**.

NEVER look directly at the sun, even if you are wearing sunglasses. It can damage your eyes.

Sunlight is **bright** when there are no clouds.

Bright light = Easy to see

4

What do you think?

Clouds in the sky sometimes block sunlight.
The clouds make the sunlight **dim**—less bright.

Dim light

Is it easier or harder to see when
light is dim?

(Answer on page 20)

5

Darkness

When there is no light, there is **darkness**.

It is dark inside this box. The box blocks the light from getting inside.

Box with lid = Dark inside

6

What do you think?

Now the box has no lid. The light can get inside the box.

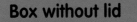

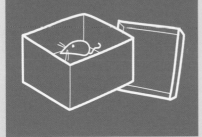

Is it light or dark in a box when you take off the lid?

(Answer on page 20)

7

Making Light

When it is dark, we can make **artificial** light by switching on a lamp or flashlight.

The light is brightest close to the lamp.

The light is dimmer farther away from the lamp.

Far from flashlight = Dim light

8

What do you think?

You can use a flashlight to read in the dark.

Close to flashlight

Is it easier or harder to see a page if you hold a flashlight very close to it?

(Answer on page 20)

Shadows

Light travels in straight lines. When an object blocks the light's path, it makes a **shadow**.

This wall blocks the light. It makes a shadow.

Different shapes make different shadows.

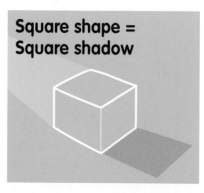

Square shape = Square shadow

What do you think?

Look at these shadows on the beach.

Round shape

What kind of shadow will this ball make?

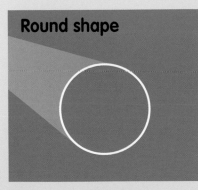

11

Sound

Sound is energy that you can hear. A shout is a loud sound.

Loud sounds travel far. People shout when they want people who are far away to hear them.

Loud sounds = Travel far

What do you think?

A whisper is a **quiet** sound. People whisper when they want only people close by to hear them.

Quiet sounds

Can you hear someone whisper if you are far away?

(Answer on page 21)

13

Vibrations

A sound is made when something **vibrates**. The vibrations travel through the air and into your ears.

The dog's ears hear vibrations. Your ears hear vibrations, too!

Vibrations = Sound

What do you think?

The boy plucks the guitar strings to make them vibrate. The vibrating strings make sounds.

What happens to the sounds when the strings stop vibrating?

No vibrations

(Answer on page 21)

15

Heard But Not Seen

Sound does not travel in a straight line, like light. Sound travels in all directions.

All the people at this parade can hear the marching band.

Fire engine = Heard and seen

What do you think?

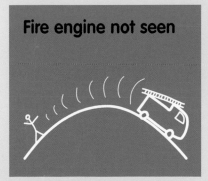

Fire engine not seen

Can you hear a fire engine
when you can't see it?

(Answer on page 21)

19

Answers

Page 5

It is harder to see when light is dim.

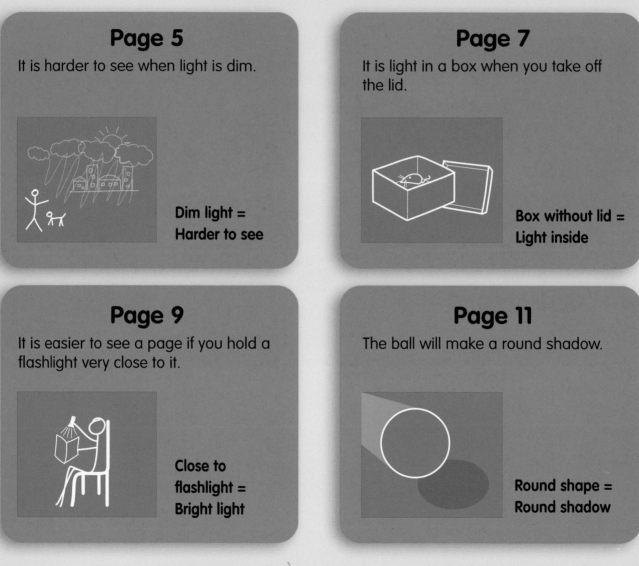

**Dim light =
Harder to see**

Page 7

It is light in a box when you take off the lid.

**Box without lid =
Light inside**

Page 9

It is easier to see a page if you hold a flashlight very close to it.

**Close to
flashlight =
Bright light**

Page 11

The ball will make a round shadow.

**Round shape =
Round shadow**

16

Page 13

You cannot hear someone whisper if you are far away.

**Quiet sounds =
Don't travel far**

Page 15

The sounds stop when the strings stop vibrating.

**No vibrations =
No sound**

Page 17

You will make a louder sound if you hit the drum harder.

**Hard hit =
Loud sound**

Page 19

You can hear a fire engine when you can't see it because sound travels in all directions.

**Fire engine
not seen =
Still heard**

Glossary

artificial (ar-ti-FISH-uhl) made by human beings

bright (BRITE) strong light that is easy to see

darkness (DARK-ness) no light

dim (DIM) weak light that is hard to see

energy (EN-ur-jee) power from different sources that makes things work or produces heat

light (LITE) a kind of energy that we see

natural (NACH-ur-uhl) made by nature

quiet (KWYE-uht)
sounds that are
not loud

sunlight (SUHN-lite)
light that comes from
the sun

shadow
(SHAD-oh)
a dark
shape
made when
something
blocks light

vibrates
(VYE-brates)
moves back
and forth
quickly

sound
(SOUND)
a kind of energy
that we hear

23

Index

Picture credits

Corbis: 1, 3, 4, 5, 6, 7, 10, 11, 14, 23.
Powerstock: front cover, 2, 8, 9,
12, 13, 15, 16, 17, 18, 19

Every effort has been made to trace the copyright holders, and we apologize in advance for any unintentional omissions. We would be pleased to insert the appropriate acknowledgments in any subsequent edition of this publication.